Creation

The Gospel Coalition Booklets
Edited by D. A. Carson & Timothy Keller

Gospel-Centered Ministry *by D. A. Carson and Timothy Keller*

The Restoration of All Things *by Sam Storms*

The Church: God's New People *by Tim Savage*

The Holy Spirit *by Kevin L. DeYoung*

Can We Know the Truth? *by Richard D. Phillips*

What Is the Gospel? *by Bryan Chapell*

The Plan *by Colin S. Smith*

Creation

Andrew M. Davis

::: CROSSWAY
WHEATON, ILLINOIS

Contents

There are two categories into which everything in the universe fits, and there is an infinite distance between the two: the Creator and creation. God alone had no beginning; he is self-existent and depends on nothing for his continued existence. Everything else in the universe was created by God and for God. In this booklet, we have the delightful work of considering the doctrine of creation, understanding its significance, and applying its truths to our lives.

The Nature of Creation: Revelation from God

All the information we have concerning the creation of the universe comes by revelation from God. The two great sources of this knowledge are the physical creation around us and the Scripture, which describes it accurately to us. From the very beginning, God crafted a universe that reveals his existence and true nature so that we would know him and worship him. Romans 1:20 asserts, "Since the creation of the world God's invisible qualities—his eternal power and divine nature—have been clearly seen, being understood from what has been made" (NIV).

The Purpose of Creation: Displaying God's Glory

God made the universe to display his glory. It was certainly not for any lack on God's part, as though God needed anything, but rather for a desire to give generously from the greatness of his being. The twenty-four elders who surround the throne in the book of Revelation are fulfilling the purpose of creation when they use it for the praise of God's glory: "Worthy are you, our Lord and God, to receive glory and honor and power, for you created all things, and by your will they existed and were created" (Rev. 4:11).

As God created the universe, he poured his glory into every atom and complex system, whether in the cosmos or in the ecosphere. As Psalm 19:1 puts it, "The heavens declare the glory of God, and the sky above proclaims his handiwork." The creation is not waiting to display the glory of God; it already does. The seraphim flying around the Lord's throne proclaim this constantly: "Holy, holy, holy is the LORD of hosts; the whole earth is full of his glory!" (Isa. 6:3).

The Purpose of Humanity: Knowing God's Glory

A prophecy by Habakkuk declares the purpose of humanity (and of redemptive history): "The earth will be filled with the knowledge of the glory of the LORD as the waters cover the sea" (Hab. 2:14). Since the earth already displays the glory of God, all that is left is for the earth to be filled with the *knowledge* of that glory. This task cannot be performed by the earth's atmosphere, the majestic cedars of Lebanon, the towering Himalayas of Nepal, soaring eagles, or powerful elks. Though all these created beings *display* the glory of God, they cannot *know* the glory of God. That vital task of worship was assigned to the human race, created in the image of God to search out both the obvious and hidden displays of God's glory in every aspect of creation.

But the immeasurable tragedy of Adam's rebellion in the garden of Eden is that the human heart, which should have delighted in God the creator, worshiped the creation instead (Rom 1:25). So while the human race has been fruitful and multiplied and in a large measure filled the earth with the image of God, the Lord's original intention—an earth filled with the knowledge of his glory—still awaits fulfillment.

There is only one force in the universe with the power to transform the idolatrous hearts of humans into those that will know the glory of the Lord as displayed in creation: the gospel of Jesus Christ. By this gospel our hearts of stone are transformed, made alive to the glory of God shining all around us. The fulfillment of this grand overarching promise awaits the new heaven and new earth, when the glory of God will illuminate every created thing and the righteous themselves will "shine like the sun in the kingdom of their Father" (Matt. 13:43).

A Personal and Global Education in Theology

Our education in theology—God's existence and attributes—began from the moment we were conceived in our mother's womb and continued day by day long before we learned language. We were educated by the sound of our mother's heartbeat, the sensation of warmth, the tastes in our mouth, the blinding flash of light at birth, the brilliance of colors, and the aromas of our bassinet and clothes. David says in Psalm 22:9, "Yet You are He who brought me forth from the womb; You made me trust when upon my mother's breasts" (NASB). When David was a nursing infant, God taught him how to trust as his mother provided for his physical needs. God was preparing David to put his trust in God for the salvation of his soul. Thus, physical creation prepares us for saving faith. As we walked as children through the beauty of a forest in the splendor of fall, breathing in deeply the musty smells of the forest floor, feeling the warm breezes of a late fall afternoon on our faces, having our breath stolen by the fiery glory of a sudden scenic vista—a magnificent mountain valley, splashed with vivid reds and golds of trees preparing for the impending winter—our hearts were being shaped for the central reality of the universe: Almighty God.

This education is going on around the world; it is not unique to one nation or one region of the earth. Psalm 19:3–4 speaks of the way the heavens are declaring the glories of God in a wordless universal language: "There is no speech, nor are there words, whose voice is not heard. Their voice goes out through all the earth, and their words to the end of the world." Physical creation is a personal education in theology for people all over this globe.

All Things Created by Christ and for Christ

Everything in heaven and on earth, visible and invisible, was created by Christ and for Christ:

> All things were made through [Christ], and without him was not anything made that was made. (John 1:3)

> He is the image of the invisible God, the firstborn of all creation. For by him all things were created, in heaven and on earth, visible and invisible, whether thrones or dominions or rulers or authorities—all things were created through him and for him. (Col. 1:15–16)

> In these last days [God] has spoken to us by his Son, whom he appointed the heir of all things, through whom also he created the world. (Heb. 1:2)

In some mysterious way God spoke the universe into existence out of nothing, and Christ was the word by which God did this powerful creative speaking (John 1:3). The universe was created *for* Christ (Col. 1:16), and God appointed Christ "heir of all things" (Heb. 1:2). So, in some astonishing way, every atom in the physical universe and every entity in the spiritual realm belongs to Christ by rights.

Even more amazing, the universe God created *depends* on Christ moment by moment for its ongoing existence: "He [Christ] is before all things, and in him all things hold together" (Col. 1:17). This pictures a needy universe that would cease to exist if Christ didn't exert his powerful will to keep it in existence. That much of this physical world can be analyzed and understood in strictly physical terms does not, in the Bible's view, vitiate the sovereign sway of God over every part of it. Biblical writers know about the water cycle, but frequently they prefer to speak of God *sending* rain, for the two modes of speaking do not cancel each other out. Owing to the force of gravity, a wounded bird falls to the ground, but no sparrow tumbles out of the heavens, according to Jesus, apart from his heavenly Father's sanction. Modern physics has identified four fundamental forces that bind everything together, but this does not prevent us from recognizing that Jesus upholds everything by his powerful word.

The Threat of Naturalism

In the final analysis, there are only two explanations for the existence of the universe: special creation by a divine being and naturalistic evolution by impersonal forces. In this strong sense of the terms, creation and evolution are mutually exclusive. The fact remains, however, that neither "creation" nor "evolution" is always used in these strong antithetical senses, and this helps to make discussion of the issues more than a little complex.

According to the Bible, God insists that sinful humanity, despite being surrounded by plain evidence of the existence and nature of the invisible God, suppresses the truth in unrighteousness (Rom. 1:18). In other words, we make a willful effort to hold down what we consider to be an ugly truth: there is a holy and all-powerful Creator to whom we are eternally accountable. Rather ironically, the point is sometimes acknowledged by atheists. Richard Dawkins asserts, "Biology is the study of complicated things that give the appearance of having been designed for a purpose."[1] In other words, one has to suppress the urge to notice that this or that was designed for a purpose!

---

[1] Richard Dawkins, *The Blind Watchmaker* (New York: Norton, 1991), 1.

It is worth recognizing that both scientists and interpreters of the Bible are far from agreed *within their own domains of inquiry*. In other words, they hold to somewhat diverse interpretations of both the scientific data and the Bible. To add to the confusion, not a few people occupy *both* roles—i.e., they are both scientists and Christian interpreters of Scripture—and such people do not always agree with their fellow scientists or with their fellow Bible interpreters.

Some examples may help. On the side of the Bible, some Christians hold to the gap theory (there is a gap of indeterminate length between Genesis 1:1 and 1:2); some hold to a day-age theory (each day of Genesis 1 represents an age); some hold to young-earth theory (each day is a twenty-four-hour day, and creation took place no more than ten thousand years ago); some hold to what might be called a literary week (each day is a twenty-four-hour day, but the entire week is meant to be a literary creation that does not pretend to tell us exactly "what happened" but aims to order the account for symbolic and theological reasons, variously understood).

Several of these theories are compatible with "theistic evolution," but that expression is itself more than a little ambiguous. In the thought of some, it presupposes evolution that is indistinguishable from a naturalistic accounting of evolution, except for the assertion that God was sovereignly if benignly presiding over evolution's unfolding (in much the same way that he providentially presides over sunshine and rain today, making it possible to say that God sends the sunshine and the rain). In the thought of others, while evolution by some kind of "natural" selection takes place (presided over by God), at various points God intervened miraculously to bring about results that could not have happened naturally (e.g., God made human beings qualitatively different from other primates: they are his image bearers, destined for eternal life).

Frankly, many Christians view one or more of these options as outside the pale and are open to only one or two of the options. For example, it is frequently argued that there is no compelling *biblical* reason to see billions and billions of years in Genesis 1. The reasons some Christians change their interpretation of that text come from outside the Bible: geologists and other scientists tell us that the evidence that the earth is billions of years old is overwhelming.

Because of these arguments, some Christians reinterpret Genesis

1 to fit the prevailing scientific stance, adopting interpretations that would never have been "found" in the text had it not been for the claims science. This result, they argue, domesticates the Bible and distorts its plain sense. Yet the issue is complicated. Long before the rise of modern science, Augustine (fourth century) asserted that the interpretation of Genesis 1 is difficult, but he argued, for what he thought were compelling biblical and theological reasons, that the universe was created instantaneously and that the creation week of Genesis 1 is a symbol-laden literary creation designed to make an array of theological points, not least the ordering of the human week and the establishment of Sabbath. In other words, some sort of literary-week theory antedates the rise of modern science.

The stakeholders of The Gospel Coalition are not on the same page with respect to all the details, but all of us insist that God alone is self-existing, that he is the creator of all, that he made everything good, that Adam and Eve were historical figures from whom the rest of the human race has sprung, and that the fundamental problem we face was introduced by human idolatry and rebellion and the curse they attracted. The reasons for holding such matters to be nonnegotiable are bound up with many passages of Scripture, not just the opening chapters of Genesis. For example, Paul tells us that God "made from *one man* every nation of mankind to live on all the face of the earth" (Acts 17:26).

On the side of science, as on the side of biblical interpretation, there is more uncertainty and diversity of opinion, at least on some of the issues, than is commonly acknowledged. Although the vast majority of scientists hold to the big bang theory, which asserts that everything in the universe was compacted into one incredibly dense body that at some point exploded in a "singularity" (i.e., an event in which the known laws of physics do not prevail) to produce, after about fifteen billion years, the universe as we know it, a minority of scientists remain suspicious. More importantly, there is no widely accepted theory about how that incredibly dense body came to exist in the first place. One theory postulates an alternately expanding and contracting universe, but the speculations involved are so extravagant that the theory has gained little traction.

If we sidestep questions about how that dense body came to be and focus instead on planet earth, we see that theories regarding the development of life along evolutionary lines have undergone repeated modification. The fossil record preserves so many gaps in the expected sequence of transitional forms that it is now common to follow the proposal of the late Harvard evolutionary theorist Stephen Jay Gould. He suggests that instead of smooth evolutionary development by natural selection, one must posit "punctuated equilibrium"; that is, evolution takes place in periodic surges of activity that were so brief they could not be captured by the fossil record. Moreover, despite the most valiant research efforts, the path from inorganic matter to a functioning and reproducing cell is still remarkably opaque on the assumptions of philosophical materialism.

Equally complex are recent debates over intelligent design. Over the past two decades or so, a small group of scientists and philosophers have argued that many biological structures are characterized by "irreducible complexity." By this they mean that for such structures to operate and be sustained (such as the eye), so many evolutionary developments would have had to take place at the same time that the statistical likelihood approaches zero. The components of the structure could not have developed piecemeal since they have no useful function apart from their place and role in the entire structure. This they take to be evidence of intelligent design.

A majority of scientists responds that this sounds like the outmoded "God of the gaps" theory: whenever science cannot explain something, we appeal to God, but the sad effect is that as science explains more and more of the "gaps," God becomes smaller and smaller. Those who defend intelligent design insist that what they are arguing is quite different: we *do* understand a great deal about these structures, and the evidence from these structures, from the science itself, is that one must factor intelligent design into the explanation.

Increasingly it has become clear that behind this debate is a fundamental dispute over the very nature of science. One side thinks of science as the set of disciplines, testable theories, repeatable procedures, measurements, and necessary inferences that enables us to make sense of and increasingly understand the nature of physical reality. Those who oppose intelligent design think of science as the set of disciplines, testable theories, repeatable procedures, measurements, and necessary inferences that enables us to make sense of and increasingly understand the nature of physical reality *not only on an exclusively materialist basis but also on the assumption that such methods and results cannot speak to the existence of anything or anyone outside the material order.*

In other words, this view of science is committed to functioning philosophical materialism. God is excluded by definition. Many scientists who hold this view are not atheists, of course, but they think that what may be known of God has no intersections with the material order, which must be allowed its investigative disciplines and results unchecked by anything outside itself.

Irony surfaces, of course, when many scientists, not a few of them atheists, speak of the order and beauty of science and numbers in reverential terms filled not only with awe but also with worship. Relatively few scientists who write on these matters treat the material order as utterly cold, the result of the statistical bumping of molecules and of atomic and sub-atomic particles.

These reflections pave the way for more focused reading of biblical texts.

Genesis 1:1: The Foundation

The first statement in the Bible is foundational to everything that follows: "In the beginning, God created the heavens and the earth" (Gen. 1:1). This teaches at least three significant truths:

1) God preexisted the universe. God was there at the beginning and acted to bring everything else about.
2) The universe had a beginning. It is not eternal (as some scientists teach) or cyclical (as some Eastern religions teach).
3) God personally created everything in the universe. Nothing arose by merely impersonal physical forces, as atheistic evolutionists teach.

The doctrine of creation is the foundation of everything that follows chronologically and theologically, and redemptive history depends on its truths.

The Unfolding of Creation Week: Genesis 1

"The earth was formless and void, and darkness was over the surface of the deep" (Gen. 1:2 NASB). This needy universe required the ongoing work of God to bring it to full order and beauty. The fact that "the Spirit of God was hovering over the face of the waters" gives a first insight into the life-giving role of the Spirit, a role progressively unpacked throughout the Bible.

Then God spoke the words of sovereign power: "'Let there be light,' and there was light" (Gen 1:3). Here we are introduced to the central force and power of God in the universe: his powerful word. It is by words that God creates and by words he rules over his creation. "By the word of the LORD the heavens were made, and by the breath of his mouth all their host" (Ps. 33:6). Then God organized the rhythms of earthly life in a cycle he labeled "day" and "night": "And there was evening and there was morning, the first day" (Gen. 1:5). This rhythm of evening and morning and the counting of days throughout Genesis 1 established a pattern of the unfolding of time as we human beings know it.

One of the foci of contemporary discussion regarding the interpretation of Genesis 1 is the meaning of the word "day." While the Hebrew word *yōm* ("day") can refer to an extended period of time, such as an epoch of history, by far the most common meanings are either the twenty-four-hour period or the period of sunlight versus the period of darkness ("day and night"). Certainly in Genesis 1 the rhythm of the repeated "And there was evening and there was morning, the first [second, third, etc.] day" argues for ordinary twenty-four-hour days. This understanding is confirmed by another passage: "For in six days the Lord made heaven and earth, the sea, and all that is in them, and rested on the seventh day. Therefore the LORD blessed the Sabbath day and made it holy" (Ex. 20:11). Of course, one must also acknowledge that if the symbol-laden theory of Augustine is adopted, or one of its contemporary equivalents, these days in Genesis 1 may well be twenty-four-hour periods as part of a literary-rhetorical structure by which creation is being interpreted.

What is clear is that intrinsic to the first three days of creation was the principle of separation—this from that: light from darkness, water above from water below, and sea from dry land. God established a seemingly fragile boundary line between the mighty ocean waves and the dry land, as anyone who has visited the beach can testify. There are sometimes signs that forbid us from walking on the sand dunes lest the dune grass be trampled and perish. The dune grass prevents erosion of the fragile shoreline, and the shoreline protects us from the raging waves. The same sort of reflection is found in God's self-disclosure to Job:

Who shut up the sea behind doors
   when it burst forth from the womb,
when I made the clouds its garment
   and wrapped it in thick darkness,
when I fixed limits for it
   and set its doors and bars in place,
when I said, "This far you may come and no farther;
   here is where your proud waves halt"? (Job 38:8–11 NIV)

Once dry land had been cleared, God had a blank canvas on which to paint the marvels of life. He spoke forth the plant life of the earth, the seed-bearing plants of every kind. The words *seed* and *kind* speak of the genetic recipe for each kind of vegetation and the power to reproduce and spread throughout the surface of the earth. Who can fail to notice the majestic variety of the vegetation on the earth? God spoke forth mighty redwoods, frail ferns, fragrant orchids, and spectacular wildflowers. God wove every living and growing thing with which he beautified the dry land into a complex biological system of plant life that would take nutrients from the soil, carbon dioxide from the air, and energy from the sun to live and grow and provide food for the animals and humans that would come later.

On the fourth day of creation, God began to spread his glories through the cosmos. Though he had created light at the very beginning, now he desired to delegate the responsibility of giving light to the earth to created entities—the sun, the moon, and the stars. All that we know of light today ultimately comes from the sun and other stars, but in the Genesis account the celestial bodies are added later. The sun is an astonishing creation—a raging inferno of power that in some ways displays God's transcendence to an arrogant human race.

There is nothing humanity can do to the sun, good or bad. We cannot make it brighter or dimmer, larger or smaller, nearer or farther, hotter or cooler. If we decided as a human race that we wanted to destroy the sun, there would be nothing we could do to it. If we amassed all our thermonuclear weapons and sent them as intergalactic rockets to explode on the surface of the sun, they would never make it but would be incinerated millions of miles away from their destination. NASA is presently planning a solar probe mission that will be able to get only within 3.5 million miles of the surface.

The sun burns on day after day without any visible diminution of its power, so bright we cannot look at it steadily without being blinded. The sun glorifies God by its astonishing power and brightness, and yet the sun was designed with human beings in mind, shining in the sky "to give light on the earth" (Gen. 1:17).

God created the moon for the same human-centered purpose, but unlike the sun it gives a borrowed light to the earth. The moon reflects the sun's light to the earth, just as in a metaphorical sense we believers will one day shine with the light of Christ in heaven. And then comes this laconic statement: "He also made the stars" (Gen. 1:16 NIV). Recent advances in cosmology, such as the Hubble Space Telescope that orbits the earth and projects back absolutely stunning images of the starry host, have shown us how immense is the universe that God has made.

On the fifth day, God filled the seas with swimming creatures and the skies with flying creatures. The incalculable variety of species of fish and birds boggles the mind to the glory of God. God created whales to be the largest living creature on earth and then opens his hand to feed them as much as 2,600 pounds of plankton every day. There are spectacularly beautiful tropical fish, sporting vivid designs that radiate with every color in the spectrum. And there are grotesque-looking fish called brotulids that can exist almost five miles below the surface of the ocean. The birds also display the staggering creativity of God, for some of them—like eagles—soar on thermals, hardly ever flapping their wings, and others—like hummingbirds—flap their wings at as many as eighty beats per second. Peregrine falcons are the fastest creatures in nature, traveling up to 240 miles per hour in vertical dives.

God blessed the fish and birds, commanding them to fill the sea and sky.

On the sixth day, God turned his attention to the dry land and brought forth the beasts of the earth—livestock, wild animals, and creatures that crawl along the earth. The complexity and variety of these species are clear testimonies to the wisdom and goodness of God. Some of the creatures are mighty and powerful, like the elephant, which can lift more than six hundred pounds with its trunk. Some are timid and tiny, like the rock badger, which dwells on mountain ledges and sucks moisture from the lichens growing on the cliffs. It was God who created the mighty lion to roar, the otter to swim, the hippopotamus to dominate the African rivers, and the cheetah to run like the wind.

The Climax of Creation: The Image of God

Having set the magnificent stage, a completed universe fully equipped with God's loving provision, the time had come for the climax of creation: the fashioning of human beings, male and female, in the image of God:

> Then God said, "Let us make man in our image, after our likeness. And let them have dominion over the fish of the sea and over the birds of the heavens and over the livestock and over all the earth and over every creeping thing that creeps on the earth." So God created man in his own image, in the image of God he created him; male and female he created them. (Gen. 1:26–27)

Humans are unique because God created them in his image. Human beings were created not to be God but to be God's image. In what does this "image" consist? There are at least two significant ways in which humanity stands as the image of God: (1) *In our nature.* We are like God in certain capabilities (ability to think, reason, plan, love, choose, desire, communicate, etc.) and attributes (righteousness, holiness, mercy, compassion, wisdom, and so forth). (2) *In our position in the world.* God established the human race as the rulers of the earth (Gen. 1:26, 28).

God's creation also establishes the pattern of gender. God created humans male and female, each equally in his image yet with distinguishable emphases and roles—all by God's design. Homosexuality and other forms of gender confusion blur the distinctions between male and female. God intended gender distinction as a good thing from the very beginning: it is a very good thing for a man to be a man and for a woman to be a woman.

God intended for the human race to multiply and fill the world with the image of God and that this multiplication be the result of his personal blessing. As God blesses male and female (i.e., husband and wife, as we learn to call them in Genesis 2), children are born, and the image of God spreads. Thus, children are a blessing from God, not the expensive and inconvenient curse some selfish people in our society think them to be.

God's loving provision for the human race and for all animals is laid out at the end of the creation account—seed-bearing plants and trees for man and green vegetables for the animals. This establishes so beautifully the sovereign providence for ongoing life. As we have mentioned, God created a needy universe, and God is greatly glorified in the creature's dependence. The goodness of God in provision of food is the theme of the psalmist's meditation in Psalm 104: "These all look to you to give them their food at the proper time. When you give it to them, they gather it up; when you open your hand, they are satisfied with good things" (vv. 27–28 NIV).

The Goodness of God in the Goodness of Creation

God completes the account of his creation of the universe with this sweeping assessment: "And God saw everything that he had made, and behold, it was very good" (Gen. 1:31). This is a vastly important declaration, for it asserts the essential goodness of physical matter. Greek philosophers and Eastern mystics have denied the goodness of the physical world and especially of the human body. God declared that everything he had made was good. Even more important than this, however, is that the creation showed God himself to be good.

We live in a universe that was intelligently and lovingly crafted by a God who is good and who loves what he has made. We live on a planet that is uniquely prepared for human life in particular. The earth travels at precisely 66,600 miles per hour as it orbits the sun. This speed is exactly what is needed to offset the sun's gravitational pull and keep the earth the proper distance from the sun for life to thrive. It was the goodness of God that set the angle of tilt of the earth's axis—23.5 degrees relative to the sun—to give a beautiful variation of seasons to the hemispheres. If the tilt were increased to 25 degrees, summer would be much hotter and winters much colder, resulting in devastation of the plant life of earth. So the speed and position of the earth were "very good" for human life.

God also finely tuned the earth's atmosphere unlike any other in the solar system. Far above our heads, ozone blocks the potentially cancer-causing radiation from the sun. The atmosphere shields the earth from meteors, burning up as much as 70,000 tons of space debris a year. It contains 78 percent nitrogen and 21 percent oxygen—just perfect for life. Without oxygen, all animate life would be unable to survive, but if the amount were increased to, say, 25 percent, fires would break out instantly all over the earth, and it would be nearly impossible to put them out. The nitrogen not only dilutes the oxygen but also provides an essential fertilizer for plant life. Amazingly, during electrical storms all over the earth, lightning bolts combine nitrogen and oxygen into compounds vital for plant life, and these compounds are then carried into the soil by the rain. And so the atmosphere is "very good" for human life.

Just before his death in May 1543, Polish astronomer Nicolaus Copernicus published his seminal book, *On the Revolution of the Celestial Spheres.* He demonstrated that the sun, rather than the earth, is the center of the solar system. Science has vindicated his views physically, but Genesis 1 still carves out a central concept that cannot be controverted biblically: the earth is the center of God's purposes for the universe. According to Genesis 1:14–18, all of the reasons that God created the sun, moon, and stars were *earth-centered* reasons: to give light to the earth; to separate day from night; to mark seasons, days, and years. The earth-central viewpoint of the cosmos is also vindicated in the book of Revelation when, as events on the surface of the earth and in human history come to a climax, the stars fall from the sky to the earth like figs shaken from a fig tree (Rev. 6:13). The earth is the centerpiece of God's plan for the universe.

The Sabbath Rest

The Genesis account of the seven days of creation closes with God's taking his Sabbath rest and establishing the Sabbath as a blessed and holy day (Gen. 2:1–3). Of course, it should never be understood that God took his Sabbath rest because his work in creating the universe had worn him out and he needed to replenish his strength. Isaiah 40:28 makes this very plain: "The LORD is the everlasting God, the Creator of the ends of the earth. He does not faint or grow weary."

Neither should we imagine that God ceased from exerting energy toward the universe that he made; God created a needy and dependent universe that relies on him at every moment for its existence. Rather, God's Sabbath rest is two things: (1) a display of his sovereign right to rule over the universe, like a king through his throne room who walks, climbs the dais, turns and faces his court, and with great solemnity sits on the throne to rule; (2) a display of his kindness to human beings, giving them an opportunity to enter God's rest in this present age, one day in seven, as well as for eternity in heaven through faith in Christ (Heb. 4:1–11).

The Special Creation of Humans: The Details of Genesis 2

Some commentators have had difficulty reconciling the different accounts of creation given in Genesis 1 and 2. However, as Charles Spurgeon once said about a different theological issue, "I never try to reconcile friends!" Genesis 2 is a perfect complement to Genesis 1. Genesis 1 gives the grand, overarching account of God's creation of the cosmos and especially his purposes in creating humans as male and female in the image of God. But Genesis 2 zeroes in with indispensable detail on the formation of the first man and woman and his special purposes for each. Genesis 1 and 2 are like a map of California with an inset map of Los Angeles on the same page.

A Glorious yet Needy Earth Waits for Its Caretaker and Ruler

Genesis 2 depicts an earth all decked out with the glory of God and yet needy and awaiting its caretaker and ruler. Although the earth was declared "very good" in Genesis 1, that doesn't mean it couldn't be developed and improved. And so Genesis 2:5 speaks of a certain category of plants that need human cultivation and husbandry to reach its full potential. Where would the first man get such skill? It would come from his heavenly Father's direct instruction; God intended to train his offspring Adam in the ways of the earth. A remarkable passage in Isaiah 28 shows the direct intervention of God in the agricultural education of man:

> When a farmer plows for planting, does he plow continually?
>> Does he keep on breaking up and harrowing the soil?
> When he has leveled the surface,
>> does he not sow caraway and scatter cummin?
> Does he not plant wheat in its place,
>> barley in its plot,
>> and spelt in its field?
> His God instructs him
>> and teaches him the right way.

Caraway is not threshed with a sledge,
> nor is a cartwheel rolled over cummin;
caraway is beaten out with a rod,
> and cummin with a stick.
Grain must be ground to make bread;
> so one does not go on threshing it forever.
Though he drives the wheels of his threshing cart over it,
> his horses do not grind it.
All this also comes from the LORD Almighty,
> wonderful in counsel and magnificent in wisdom. (Isa. 28:24–29 NIV)

The First Man Created a Living Creature

Genesis 2:7 relates the special creation of the first man from the dust of the earth: "The LORD God formed the man of dust from the ground and breathed into his nostrils the breath of life, and the man became a living creature." I remember seeing an exhibit in the Boston Museum of Science that showed the outline of a man, and inside the outline were a series of chemical bottles of varying sizes filled with dry compounds. It represented a human body from which all water had been removed (the human body is over 60 percent water), and what was left were a bunch of chemical compounds and minerals, all of which can be mined from the earth! The first man was of the earth, earthy (1 Cor. 15:47 KJV), and after the fall into sin, God told Adam that he would die and return to the earth, since from it "you were taken; for you are dust, and to dust you shall return" (Gen. 3:19).

Yet as earthy as we are, it is still staggering to the mind to meditate on the complexity of the human body, which God fearfully and wonderfully fashions from those various earthy compounds (Ps. 139:14). Modern genetic science tells us that the DNA found in the trillions of cells in a single human being, if unraveled from that complex double-helix found in every cell and placed end-to-end, would travel 10 to 20 billion miles. How much more astonishing is the marvel of the human brain, which is the most complex physical thing God ever created, having one hundred billion neurons (approximately the same number as trees in the Amazonian jungle)?

The Special Commands of God

Though God had fashioned a whole world filled with his glory, the Lord had specially prepared a place for Adam and his wife to begin their thrilling journey of exploration and development. It was "in the east, in Eden" (Gen. 2:8 NIV), and there God placed the man he had formed. God had richly supplied the garden of Eden with every kind of fruitful tree, beautiful to the eye, pleasing to the palate. In the center of the garden was the tree of life. Also in the garden was the tree of the knowledge of good and evil. These trees were the focus of the special commands God was about to entrust to Adam.

Genesis 2:10–14 describes four rivers, the origin of which was in the garden of Eden (and rather surprising archaeological discoveries continue to be made concerning these rivers). Genesis 2:15 follows: "The LORD God took the man and put him in the garden of Eden to work it and keep it." The Hebrew verbs "work" and "keep" are very common words in the Old Testament, and their root meaning is something like "serve" and "protect." Adam was to serve the garden of Eden by his labor, exerting himself to bring it to its full potential under the tutelage of his heavenly Father. The herbs and other cultivated plants mentioned in Genesis 2:5 would receive the care they needed to grow. The second command, to protect, implies that impending danger threatened the beauty and peace of Eden. This danger is made obvious in Genesis 3, where Satan comes in the form of a serpent to tempt Eve and Adam and lead them (and the garden of Eden) into death.

Having placed Adam in Eden, God then gave him this clear command: "You may surely eat of every tree of the garden, but of the tree of the knowledge of good and evil you shall not eat, for in the day that you eat of it you shall surely die" (Gen. 2:16–17). Here God places Adam under a restriction. This is law, warning, limitation. Adam is given charge of the whole earth to rule it, but Adam himself must submit to God.

The Creation of Eve and Marriage

Male and female humans are each created in the image of God and charged to be fruitful, multiply, and fill the earth (Gen. 1:26–27). But Adam is created alone and walks alone for a time. Though God declared that it was not good for Adam to remain alone (Gen. 2:18), it was no accident that God created him first and allowed him to be alone for a brief period. God did this to establish Adam as the head of his wife and to display her role as "a helper suitable for him" (Gen. 2:18 NIV; see 1 Cor. 11:2–16; Eph. 5:22–33; 1 Tim. 2:11–15).

After Adam names the animals (Gen. 2:19–20), it is clear that among them there is no helper suitable for him. Adam could not be fruitful alone, nor could he love and relate to another as one in the image of God was designed to do. So God caused a deep sleep to come on Adam, and he took a rib from that man and formed a woman from the rib while the man was sleeping. God brought her to the man and presented her to him to be his wife. In poetic voice, Adam rejoices: "This at last is bone of my bones and flesh of my flesh; she shall be called Woman, for she was taken out of Man" (v. 23).

In naming her, Adam shows his authority in marriage, but in his celebration of her essential sameness with him, he shows the partnership they would have as created equally in the image of God. This was the origin of marriage, the first human relationship in the Bible, and the pattern of all future marriages. It is also a picture of Christ and the church (Eph. 5:32). Before they sinned against God, they were so free that they "were both naked and were not ashamed" (Gen. 2:25); neither had anything to hide, so unlike the wretched situation that prevails once sin has conquered them.

A Tragic Fall for Creation

The creation that surrounds us is very different from the perfect world that surrounded Adam and Eve in Eden. Adam, representing the human race, failed *to serve and protect* his wife or the garden of Eden. He stood idly by while Satan tempted his wife, and then he followed her into open rebellion by eating from the tree of the knowledge of good and evil (Gen 3:1–7).

God came as the judge of all the earth and confronted first Adam, then Eve, then the Serpent. He cursed all three in turn, and with Adam's curse the earth itself was cursed: "Cursed is the ground because of you; in pain you shall eat of it all the days of your life; thorns and thistles it shall bring forth for you; and you shall eat the plants of the field" (Gen. 3:17–18).

Since that time, creation has groaned in bondage to corruption and futility, longing for the glorious completion of human salvation (Rom. 8:18–22). We see the evidence of that groaning, bondage, corruption, and futility every day, and we ourselves yearn for the day when creation will be free to be perfect and glorious again.

The New Creation

The gospel of Jesus Christ has unleashed the power of God to bring that day about. A new era in human history began with Christ's resurrection. Christ's resurrection body—a "spiritual body"—is the prototype for a new universe. He is the "firstfruits" from the dead (1 Cor. 15:20, 23). As the gospel of Christ's redeeming death and glorious resurrection makes its way around the world, sinful descendants of Adam are repenting and believing in Christ and finding redemption in him. At that instant they are made "new creations" in Christ spiritually (2 Cor. 5:17), and they begin to long to be made new creations physically as well.

So both Christians and the universe groan inwardly as we await eagerly our final redemption, the resurrection of our bodies (Rom. 8:23). At the second coming of Christ, this fervent hope will be fulfilled, and the creation itself will be made new. The universe, spiritual and physical, will in some sense be resurrected like our bodies, so there will be continuity and difference. And that new universe has a glorious name, "a new heaven and a new earth, the home of righteousness" (2 Pet. 3:13).

Applications of the Doctrine of Creation

The doctrine of creation should open our eyes to the glories of God around us and should enable us to have an endless stream of reasons to praise and worship God. We should be ready to give God thanks for the beauty of the earth, for its display of his goodness and love, for its variety, for its sweet provision of all of our needs, despite all the signs of the curse that afflict it.

Not only does all creation display the power of God the creator, but, like David in Psalm 139, we should marvel that God personally wove us together in our mother's womb and sustains us every moment of our lives. We should understand that in God "we live and move and have our being" (Acts 17:28). We should know that God holds in his hand our lives and all our ways (Dan. 5:23). This should move us to the kind of awe-struck intimacy with God that David displays in Psalm 139: "Search me, O God, and know my heart!" (v. 23).

Our regeneration is like what God did at the very beginning of creation: "For God, who said, 'Let light shine out of darkness,' has shone in our hearts to give the light of the knowledge of the glory of God in the face of Jesus Christ" (2 Cor. 4:6). This clearly displays the absolute sovereignty of God in our conversion. Just as God spoke into the dark nothingness at creation saying, "Let there be light," and there was light, so God spoke into the dark nothingness of our hearts to create a new spiritual light—the light of Christ. That is what regeneration is, and only the sovereign God can do it. And when God wills to do it, no power in the universe can stop it!

Creation is the simplest and clearest starting place for parents to teach little ones about the existence and attributes of God. Parents should saturate their own language with words of praise and thanksgiving to God the creator constantly and then seek those spiritual analogies mentioned in the previous point to teach their children the gospel of Jesus Christ.

Many books of the Bible begin their presentation of gospel truth with the doctrine of creation (e.g., Genesis, John, Romans, Colossians, Hebrews). This is a point of contact we can make with a biblically illiterate world. As we seek to take the gospel to the ends of the earth to unreached people groups, inevitably the starting point of our proclamation will be creation. This is increasingly true in our own culture as well, as fewer and fewer people in the Western world know the Scriptures. Also the gospel message itself should be tied intimately to creation.

The earth was entrusted to us by its Creator, and we are therefore merely stewards of someone else's possession. We should respect the earth as a creation of our heavenly Father and take care of it lovingly. We should *serve* and *protect* the earth, bringing it to its full potential under God, without worshiping creation.

All believers called to study science should do so as worshipers above all else. Scientists should see their work as uncovering the marvels of God the creator, making those marvels available to their brothers and sisters for the purpose of worship and for the benefit of humanity. Scientists should not surrender their commitment to the truth of the Bible while they uncover new truths in creation.

The Bible is the greatest and clearest revelation of God's mind to the human race, but the Bible itself is unintelligible apart from the creation that surrounds us. The Bible speaks to us in the language of this world, using physical analogies to teach us spiritual truths. Jesus does this all the time: "Consider the lilies of the field" (Matt. 6:28); "The wind blows where it wishes, and you hear its sound. . . . So it is with everyone who is born of the Spirit" (John 3:8); "The kingdom of heaven is like yeast that a woman took and mixed into a large amount of flour until it worked all through the dough" (Matt. 13:33 NIV).

As we go through life in this sin-cursed world, we can easily become weary and discouraged. Psalm 23 says, "He restores my soul" (v. 3). So often God does that by the refreshing power of his creation. Make excursions into nature a regular part of your walk with Christ. Go to the seashore and listen to the pounding surf. Climb a mountain and watch the soaring eagles ride the thermals. Travel to the Grand Canyon and have your breath taken away by its immensity and dazzling colors. Let God's creation refresh your soul.

Romans 8 speaks of a Christian's hope in the resurrection of the body and by implication of the universe, as well. Live your life in fervent hope for the coming new creation. Yearn for it, pray for it, live for it, and speed its coming by evangelizing the lost.

The Gospel Coalition

The Gospel Coalition is a fellowship of evangelical churches deeply committed to renewing our faith in the gospel of Christ and to reforming our ministry practices to conform fully to the Scriptures. We have become deeply concerned about some movements within traditional evangelicalism that seem to be diminishing the church's life and leading us away from our historic beliefs and practices. On the one hand, we are troubled by the idolatry of personal consumerism and the politicization of faith; on the other hand, we are distressed by the unchallenged acceptance of theological and moral relativism. These movements have led to the easy abandonment of both biblical truth and the transformed living mandated by our historic faith. We not only hear of these influences; we see their effects. We have committed ourselves to invigorating churches with new hope and compelling joy based on the promises received by grace alone through faith alone in Christ alone.

We believe that in many evangelical churches a deep and broad consensus exists regarding the truths of the gospel. Yet we often see the celebration of our union with Christ replaced by the age-old attractions of power and affluence or by monastic retreats into ritual, liturgy, and sacrament. What replaces the gospel will never promote a mission-hearted faith anchored in enduring truth working itself out in unashamed discipleship eager to stand the tests of kingdom calling and sacrifice. We desire to advance along the King's highway, always aiming to provide gospel advocacy, encouragement, and education so that current- and next-generation church leaders are better equipped to fuel their ministries with principles and practices that glorify the Savior and do good to those for whom he shed his life's blood.

We want to generate a unified effort among all peoples—an effort that is zealous to honor Christ and multiply his disciples, joining in a true coalition for Jesus. Such a biblically grounded and united mission is the only enduring future for the church. This reality compels us to stand with others who are stirred by the conviction that the mercy of God in Jesus Christ is our only hope of eternal salvation. We desire to champion this gospel with clarity, compassion, courage, and joy—gladly linking hearts with fellow believers across denominational, ethnic, and class lines.

Our desire is to serve the church we love by inviting all of our brothers and sisters to join us in an effort to renew the contemporary church in the ancient gospel of Christ so that we truly speak and live for him in a way that clearly communicates to our age. We intend to do this through the ordinary means of his grace: prayer, the ministry of the Word, baptism and the Lord's Supper, and the fellowship of the saints. We yearn to work with all who, in addition to embracing the confession and vision set out here, seek the lordship of Christ over the whole of life with unabashed hope in the power of the Holy Spirit to transform individuals, communities, and cultures.